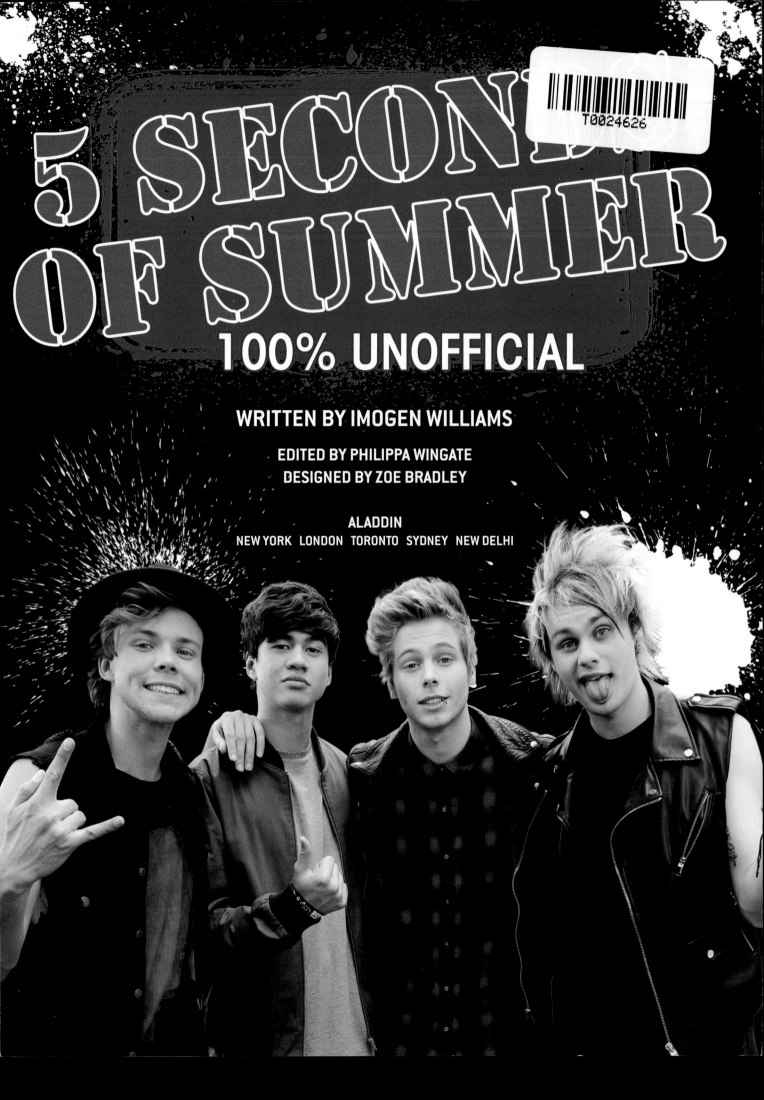

5 SECONDS OF SUMMER

100% UNOFFICIAL

WRITTEN BY IMOGEN WILLIAMS

EDITED BY PHILIPPA WINGATE
DESIGNED BY ZOE BRADLEY

ALADDIN
NEW YORK LONDON TORONTO SYDNEY NEW DELHI

INTRODUCING 5 SECONDS OF SUMMER

Get ready for 5 Seconds of Summer, the hottest new band on the block. These four Aussie guys are taking the world by storm. And they aren't just pretty faces—they are a seriously talented bunch who play their own instruments and write their own songs.

THE 5SOS JOURNEY

Luke Hemmings, Ashton Irwin, Michael Clifford, and Calum Hood began their journey recording videos and posting them on YouTube. The band was becoming an online phenomenon, and, when One Direction mentioned them on Twitter, their status rocketed. Suddenly their songs and good looks were gaining them thousands of fans around the world.

Since then, 5SOS has toured with 1D, and life has become a whirlwind of gigs, interviews, and photo shoots. Their debut album went to number one in sixty-nine countries, introducing the whole world to their unique brand of pop-rock music.

THE 5SOS FAM

The band knows they wouldn't be where they are today if it wasn't for the loyal support of their fans. The dedication of the 5SOS family (or "fam") is second to none. All around

the world, devoted fans will wait for hours outside venues just to catch a glimpse of the boys. "You are all amazing people, and so supportive," tweeted Ashton to the fans, and Calum added, "You are the best!"

BACKSTAGE PASS

This book gives you access to the boys and their music. It's packed full of great 5SOS facts and gorgeous glossy photos for you to feast your eyes on.

HELLO, GOOD LUKING

FACT FILE

NAME:
Luke Robert Hemmings

DATE OF BIRTH:
July 16, 1996

STAR SIGN:
Cancer

FAVORITE FOOD:
Pepperoni pizza

FAVORITE COLOR:
Blue

BIGGEST INSPIRATION:
Billie Joe Armstrong

LIKES:
Lip piercings, performing

DISLIKES:
Loud chewing

CELEB CRUSHES:
Jennifer Lawrence and Mila Kunis

IN LUKE'S OWN WORDS:
What word does Luke use to describe his fans?
Fabulous

What does Luke do on his days off?
Sleep as much as possible

Which actor would Luke choose to play him in a film?
Morgan Freeman

ONE THING NOBODY KNOWS ABOUT LUKE:
He carries a hairbrush with him wherever he goes.

DID YOU KNOW?
• If Luke could duet with any band, it would be Blink 182.

• Luke's the tallest member of the band.

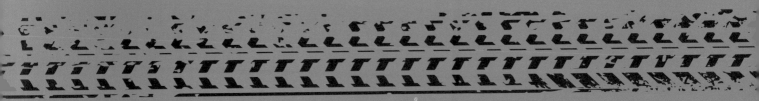

MAD FOR MICHAEL

FACT FILE

NAME:
Michael Gordon Clifford

DATE OF BIRTH:
November 20, 1995

STAR SIGN:
Scorpio .

FAVORITE FOOD:
Poppadoms

FAVORITE COLOR:
Blue

BIGGEST INSPIRATION:
Alex Gaskarth

LIKES:
Crazy hair, reality TV shows

DISLIKES:
When people don't look him in the eye
when they talk to him

CELEB CRUSH:
Ariana Grande

IN MICHAEL'S OWN WORDS:
What word does Michael use to
describe his fans?
Dedicated

What does Michael do on his days off?
Dance

Which actor would Michael choose to play
him in a film?
Zac Efron

ONE THING NOBODY KNOWS ABOUT MICHAEL:
He washes his hands about twenty times
every day!

DID YOU KNOW?
• Michael's natural hair color is blond.

• His favorite word is "cheeseburger."

CUTE CALUM

FACT FILE

NAME:
Calum Thomas Hood

DATE OF BIRTH:
January 25, 1996

STAR SIGN:
Aquarius

FAVORITE FOOD:
Spaghetti

FAVORITE COLOR:
Baby blue

BIGGEST INSPIRATION:
Green Day

LIKES:
Tea, Will Smith, and R&B

DISLIKES:
Any cheese that isn't cheddar

CELEB CRUSH:
Katy Perry

IN CALUM'S OWN WORDS:
What word does Calum use to describe his fans?
Fashionistas

What does Calum do on his days off?
Sleep and eat

Which actor would Calum choose to play him in a film?
Seth Rogen

ONE THING NOBODY KNOWS ABOUT CALUM:
He does squats every day to keep fit.

DID YOU KNOW?
• Calum had a promising soccer career before joining the band and his favorite soccer team is Liverpool FC.

• His favorite film is *Monsters, Inc.*

IT'S ALL ABOUT ASHTON

FACT FILE

NAME:
Ashton Fletcher Irwin

DATE OF BIRTH:
July 7, 1994

STAR SIGN:
Cancer

FAVORITE FOOD:
Spaghetti

FAVORITE COLOR:
Red

BIGGEST INSPIRATION:
Tré Cool

LIKES:
Love letters, hats, broccoli, and dogs

DISLIKES:
Olives, ducks, and triple chins

CELEB CRUSHES:
Hayley Williams and Mila Kunis

IN ASHTON'S OWN WORDS:
What word does Ashton use to describe his fans?
Excited

What does Ashton do on his days off?
Eat and go out in the evenings

Which actor would Ashton choose to play him in a film?
Jack Black

ONE THING NOBODY KNOWS ABOUT ASHTON:
He keeps his shoes lined up.

DID YOU KNOW?
• **Ashton loves vanilla-scented candles.**

• **He used to be in a band called Swallow the Goldfish.**

WORD SEARCH

The words hidden in the word search below are titles of 5 Seconds of Summer's bestselling songs. Can you find them all? The words might run up, down, forward, backward, or diagonally. Check your answers on page 24.

L	R	I	G	K	A	E	R	B	T	R	A	E	H	E	S	G	I	G	S	A
A	F	D	W	J	P	N	V	C	I	T	D	E	S	Z	G	R	R	N	J	M
Y	T	B	E	S	I	D	E	Y	O	U	K	F	I	V	E	E	J	H	P	N
E	H	T	C	Z	I	K	D	N	W	T	I	G	S	A	O	E	L	R	T	E
L	E	H	Q	P	B	G	K	C	S	U	S	N	T	E	C	N	K	B	E	S
T	Y	N	R	M	X	H	O	I	D	W	S	U	A	V	I	L	A	R	D	I
H	I	G	O	F	V	B	J	O	G	K	M	T	S	E	O	I	L	P	Q	A
U	N	R	M	I	S	E	G	I	D	N	E	G	O	R	E	G	D	S	A	M
E	S	N	E	V	E	R	B	E	R	G	K	W	G	B	E	H	O	P	X	T
L	H	J	A	U	O	Y	S	I	A	G	I	H	K	E	R	T	N	S	R	P
B	E	O	S	F	D	E	B	K	O	A	S	R	D	H	I	K	A	Y	I	E
A	L	W	G	R	E	N	I	T	H	M	S	F	L	E	B	C	H	M	L	O
T	G	H	R	U	Y	V	I	P	D	O	M	Z	A	S	R	A	S	H	T	J
C	N	O	S	A	E	R	Y	L	N	O	E	H	T	O	R	H	E	A	K	N
I	F	A	H	J	I	O	M	L	A	S	T	B	R	D	M	E	U	L	T	P
D	G	P	A	N	D	F	N	R	E	V	O	F	Y	N	A	E	S	I	A	J
E	H	S	H	E	L	O	O	K	S	S	O	P	E	R	F	E	C	T	O	K
R	A	V	B	X	D	I	T	N	D	C	A	L	H	L	G	H	D	O	N	E
P	T	E	A	P	R	E	D	I	T	I	E	K	I	S	S	M	A	H	L	L
N	D	A	L	U	M	R	H	U	Y	O	U	C	D	M	A	O	T	G	Y	G
U	H	T	O	V	E	R	A	N	D	O	V	E	R	I	H	N	L	P	T	A

SHE LOOKS SO PERFECT   THE ONLY REASON   HEARTBREAK GIRL

NEVER BE   GOOD GIRLS   AMNESIA   GREENLIGHT   BESIDE YOU

UNPREDICTABLE   OVER AND OVER   KISS ME KISS ME   TRY HARD

MAKING MUSIC

BACK IN THE BEGINNING

Luke, Michael, and Calum all met at school, and they started uploading videos of popular songs onto YouTube in February 2011. The boys soon realized that they needed a superhot drummer to complete their band, and luckily Michael knew just the guy. Ashton joined in December 2011, and before long 5SOS had dedicated fans all over the world.

MAKING THE MUSIC

What makes these guys so talented is the fact that they write all their own music and play their own instruments. Ashton has revealed that they've made up the verb "banding" to describe what they do.

At first, the band covered popular songs, but then Calum started songwriting, and before long the other boys realized they could compose their own music.

TOOLS OF THE TRADE

Michael's first guitar was an Epiphone Les Paul. Now he has a whole collection, including two Joan Jett Signature Melody Makers, a Les Paul Signature "T" Goldtop, and a Slash Signature. He has said that if he could play any other instrument, it would be the flute.

WHO SAID IT?

Can you figure out which band member said what? The answers are on page 24.

1. "I would camp out for a year to see Green Day."

2. "So excited to rock out tonight, I missed it so much."

3. "I love our tour bus."

4. "Good Charlotte is the reason I started playing guitar."

Learning another instrument would be quite an achievement, because between composing, practicing, and performing, there isn't much time left for anything else.

ROCK OR POP?

5SOS describes themselves as a rock band, and rightly so. Their influences range from Green Day to Blink 182 and All Time Low. Whatever you do, don't describe them as a boy band! There are no matching outfits and dance routines—the guys just spend all their time rocking out onstage with their guitars.

While the boys may have pop-star good looks, their fashion sense is definitely punky. They love black skinny jeans, graphic tees, and messy hair.

ROLLER COASTER RIDE

These days 5SOS gigs are epic events and sell out in minutes, but only a handful of fans turned up to their first gig. The band admits that it wasn't the best show they've ever given. Nevertheless, Ashton says it is his favorite gig because it was the beginning of their incredible journey.

The guys all agree that being in a band is their dream job. Ever since they were little they wanted to work in the music industry, but never imagined their dreams would come true. And now, thanks to the boys' hard work and the support of you, their loyal fans, 5SOS is going from strength to strength.

THE BIG QUIZ

Are you a true 5SOS superfan? Take this quiz to test your knowledge, and then check your answers on page 24.

1. WHAT'S THE NAME OF LUKE'S DOG?

a)   Dolly
b)   Molly
c)   Polly

2. HOW MANY TIMES DID 5SOS HAVE TO RIDE THE ROLLER COASTER TO FILM THE "TRY HARD" VIDEO?

a)   Seven
b)   Three
c)   Ten

3. WHAT IS THE FIRST THING THE BOYS NOTICE ABOUT A GIRL?

a)   Hairstyle
b)   Fashion sense
c)   Eye color

4. WHAT JOB DID ASHTON HAVE BEFORE JOINING THE BAND?

a)   Waiter
b)   Washing cars
c)   Working in a video store

5. WHERE DID LUKE, MICHAEL, AND CALUM FIRST MEET?

a)   At school
b)   At a gig
c)   At a band audition

6. WHICH MEMBER OF ONE DIRECTION FIRST TWEETED ABOUT 5SOS?

a)   Harry
b)   Louis
c)   Niall

7. WHERE WOULD THE BOYS MOST LIKE TO BE IF THEY COULD GO ANYWHERE FOR THE DAY?

a)   The beach
b)   New York City
c)   Home

8. WHAT'S THE MOST EMBARRASSING THING TO HAPPEN TO CALUM ONSTAGE?

a)   He ripped his pants.
b)   He fell over.
c)   He forgot the words to a song.

9. HOW DID MICHAEL BREAK HIS ARM?

a)   Skateboarding
b)   Falling off a trampoline
c)   Tripping over onstage

10. WHO DO THE BOYS SAY SPENDS THE MOST TIME ON HIS PHONE?

a)   Calum
b)   Luke
c)   Michael

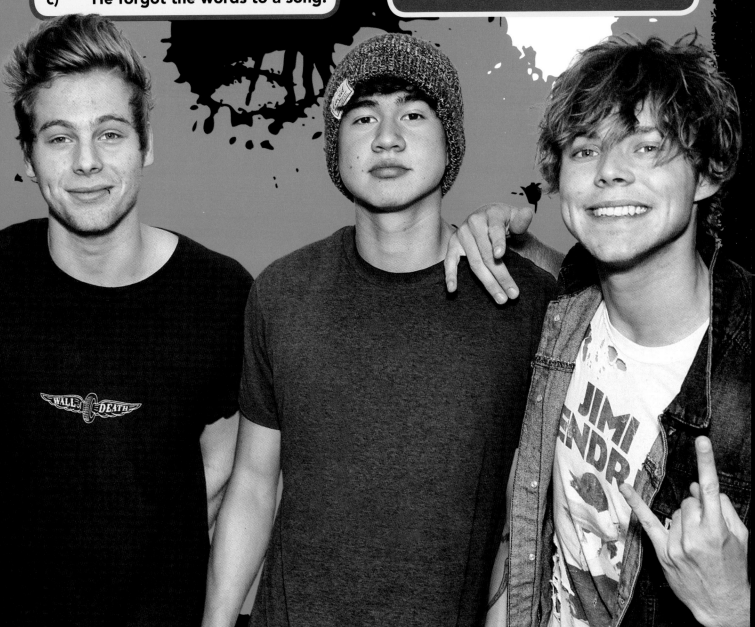

ANSWERS

Page 19: WORD SEARCH

L	R	I	G	K	A	E	R	B	T	R	A	E	H	E	S	C	I	G	S	A
A	F	D	W	J	P	N	V	C	I	T	D	E	S	Z	G	R	R	N	J	M
Y	T	B	E	S	I	D	E	Y	O	U	K	F	I	V	E	E	J	H	P	N
E	H	T	C	Z	I	K	D	N	W	T	I	G	S	A	O	E	L	R	T	E
L	E	H	Q	P	B	C	K	C	S	U	S	N	T	E	C	N	K	B	E	S
T	Y	N	R	M	X	H	O	I	D	W	S	U	A	V	I	L	A	R	D	I
H	I	G	O	F	V	B	J	O	G	K	M	T	S	E	O	I	L	P	Q	A
U	N	R	M	I	S	E	G	I	D	N	E	G	O	R	E	G	D	S	A	M
E	S	N	E	V	E	R	B	E	R	C	K	W	G	B	E	H	O	P	X	T
L	H	J	A	U	O	Y	S	I	A	G	H	K	E	R	T	N	S	R	P
B	E	O	S	F	D	E	B	K	O	A	S	R	D	H	I	K	A	T	I	E
A	L	W	G	R	E	N	I	T	H	M	S	F	L	E	B	C	H	M	L	O
T	G	H	R	U	Y	V	I	P	D	O	M	Z	A	S	R	A	S	H	T	J
C	N	O	S	A	E	R	Y	L	N	O	E	H	T	O	R	H	E	A	K	N
	F	A	H	J	I	O	M	L	A	S	T	B	R	D	M	E	U	L	T	P
D	G	P	A	N	D	F	N	R	E	V	O	F	Y	N	A	E	S	I	A	J
E	H	S	H	E	L	O	O	K	S	S	O	P	E	R	F	E	C	T	O	K
R	A	V	B	X	D	I	T	N	D	C	A	L	H	L	G	H	D	O	N	E
P	T	E	A	P	R	E	D	I	T	I	E	K	I	S	S	M	A	H	L	L
N	D	A	L	U	M	R	H	U	Y	O	U	C	D	M	A	O	T	G	Y	G
U	H	T	O	V	E	R	A	N	D	O	V	E	R	I	H	N	L	P	T	A

Page 21: WHO SAID IT?

1. Calum 2. Ashton 3. Michael 4. Luke

Pages 22–23: THE BIG QUIZ

1. b 2. a 3. b 4. c 5. a 6. b 7. c 8. a
9. b 10. c

ALADDIN
An imprint of Simon & Schuster Children's Publishing Division
1230 Avenue of the Americas, New York, New York 10020
First Aladdin paperback edition November 2014
Copyright © 2014 by Buster Books
Published by arrangement with Michael O'Mara Books Limited
ALADDIN is a trademark of Simon & Schuster, Inc., and related logo is
a registered trademark of Simon & Schuster, Inc.
For information about special discounts for bulk purchases, please contact
Simon & Schuster Special Sales at 1-866-506-1949 or business@simonandschuster.com.
The Simon & Schuster Speakers Bureau can bring authors to your live event. For more
information or to book an event contact the Simon & Schuster Speakers Bureau at
1-866-248-3049 or visit our website at www.simonspeakers.com.
Manufactured in the United States of America 1014 LAK
2 4 6 8 10 9 7 5 3 1
Library of Congress Control Number 2014950554
ISBN 978-1-4814-4365-4

PLEASE NOTE: This book is not affiliated with or endorsed by
5 Seconds of Summer or any of their publishers or licensees.

PHOTO CREDITS

Front cover: IBL / Rex Features
Back cover: Larry Busacca / Billboard Awards 2014 / Getty Images for DCP
Large poster: James McCauley / Rex Features

Page 1: Larry Busacca / Billboard Awards 2014 / Getty Images for DCP;
pages 2–3: James McCauley / Rex Features; pages 4–5: David Fisher / Rex Features;
pages 6–7: Larry Busacca / Billboard Awards 2014 / Getty Images for DCP;
page 9: Chance Yeh / FilmMagic / Getty Images; page 11: Chance Yeh / FilmMagic / Getty Images;
page 13: Kristin Callahan / Ace Pictures / Rex Features; page 15: Broadimage / Rex Features;
pages 16–17: Michael Tran / FilmMagic / Getty Images;
page 18: Shirlaine Forrest / WireImage / Getty Images; page 20: MediaPunch / Rex Features;
pages 22–23: MediaPunch / Rex Features; page 24: McPix Ltd / Rex Features
background graphics: ShutterStock Inc.